Professor Birdsong's

LAW SCHOOL GUIDE

Techniques for Choosing and Applying to Law School

Leonard Birdsong

Professor Birdsong's LAW SCHOOL GUIDE: Techniques for Choosing, and Applying to Law School

by: Leonard Birdsong

ISBN: 978-0-9898452-9-8

Winghurst Publications
1969 S. Alafaya Trail / Suite 303
Orlando, FL 32828-8732
www.BirdsongsLaw.com
lbirdsong@barry.edu

Disclaimer:
This work is based on the author's opinions and insights concerning choosing and applying to law school. Its aim is to inform and encourage those students who may be uncertain which career path they may choose in life. The author expresses herein his own views and opinions gained in his twenty years of legal teaching, serving on and chairing law school admissions committees, and working with members of the Law School Admission Council. The author's views do not reflect the official policy or position of any Law school, Law firm or other organization with which the author may have once been or may be presently affiliated. The opinions and observations provided herein are not intended to malign or defame any religion, ethnic group, club, organization, company, individual or anyone or anything. The author further covenants and represents that the work contains no matter that will incite prejudice, amount to an invasion of privacy, be libelous, obscene or otherwise unlawful or which infringe upon any proprietary interest at common law, trademark, and trade secret, patent or copyright. The author is the sole proprietor of the work and all parts thereof.

Permissions: ©Pixelrobot|Dreamstime.com
Cover Design: Rik Feeney / **www.RickFeeney.com**

Dedication

This book is dedicated to all of the law students I have had the honor of teaching over the last twenty years and to the readers of this book who may choose to enter the legal profession.

Professor Leonard Birdsong

Acknowledgments

First and foremost, I wish to acknowledge my friend, Rik Feeney, my book consultant who has taught me how to write better and how to publish my own work. Rik has also been my editor on the manuscript for this book. Thanks so much, Rik. I always learn from you.

I also wish to acknowledge my friend and colleague Katherine Sutcliffe-Lenart whose encouragement, editorial assistance and insightful criticisms and comments have helped me along the way to make this book a reality.

Table of Contents

Introduction

You may be in college or out of college uncertain what you want to do with your life. You may have toyed with the idea of going to law school. However, you're just not sure law school would be a good career choice. Reading this book may help you decide whether the benefits of a legal education could be a good career choice for you. The benefits of a legal education include being a learned professional who is looked up to by many in our society, a professional who may help clients solve their legal problems, a professional who may enter politics and help write our laws, a professional who may become wealthy, and you will be part of a profession that will never go out of business. A democratic society will always need lawyers.

I wrote this book after a wonderful career that allowed me to become a federal prosecutor in Washington, D.C., a U.S. State Department Officer who was, for a time, a hearing officer in Germany for former Nazi Party members and Waffen-SS soldiers

9

who sought visas to visit the U.S., and, while in private practice, I represented thirty-one people charged with First Degree Murder. I am now a law professor who has the honor of training new lawyers for a profession that has been good to me.

I wrote this book having been active as the Chair of and a member of law school admission committees over the years. My thoughts and observations are meant to give guidance and encouragement to current and prospective law students who may choose the legal profession as their path in life. I have had the honor over the years of working with and learning much about the law school admissions process from members of the Law School Admission Council. Information that might supplement much of what is written herein may be found online at lsac.org.

Blake Morant, President of the American Association of Law Schools (AALS) wrote in the AALS newsletter that these are challenging times for legal education since the Great Recession of 2008, when law school applications declined amid an increasingly competitive job market for law graduates. So why create more lawyers? Morant and I agree the complexity of a modern day global market demands outstanding lawyers who can represent their clients and confront and shape the most significant issues of the day. A good legal education produces well-trained professionals with critical-thinking and creative problem-solving skills. We both agree there remains a great demand for legal representation for the under-served throughout our nation. Finally, most law schools are moving forward with innovations that include an increasing number of externships, a growing focus on experiential learning, and more international opportunities.

Despite recent doom and gloom over the decline in law school applications there will always be people attracted to this noble profession. Professors like myself will be there to help train and help shape the careers of those who choose the legal profession.

Those of you who read this book and choose to go to law school will find that you have entered a profession that can bring you prestige, well-being, and a lifetime career where you may, often, be your own boss.

Chapter One
The First Lawyers?

History

Some will tell you lawyering is the second oldest profession in the world. Second behind the oldest profession in the world – prostitution. Don't believe it. Scholars trace the concept of lawyering – or advocating on behalf of others for a fee back to Fifth Century B.C.E. Greece. In Fifth Century B.C.E. Grecian society had become a very sophisticated civilization. There were many learned men who sought answers to many of the philosophical notions of the day. There were several discussions every day in the *Agora,* which was the market place of many Grecian cities, by groups of men who did not have to work because they owned land and had slaves to work for them. Their philosophical discussions centered on such notions as, did night come from day; does bad come from good; can evil be prevented by good; will the sun always rise in the east?

As a result of these discussions a cult of philosophers known as the "Sophists" came into being. Sophists were men of some learning and bearing who were good at arguing both sides of a proposition. Many of these sophists would go to the *Agora* each day and advertise their advocacy skills to the men who wished to debate philosophical notions but were not good at it themselves. For a small fee a man might pay a sophist to argue on his behalf against an opponent the notion that good comes from evil. As a result of their rhetorical skills the sophists always won the debates. However, the real skill of the sophists was the next day he could be paid a fee by another patron to argue the opposite. The sophist would argue that evil actually derives from good. They would again win the day because of their rhetorical skill.

Unfortunately, sophists came to have a bad reputation and eventually fell out of favor despite their rhetorical skills. Many people began to dislike them because the sophists appeared to have no true beliefs except that any philosophical position could be argued and won. The sophists of old are gone.

However, the words "sophist" and "sophistry" have become in modern times derogatory words which means a person who speaks out of both sides of his/her mouth, has no true convictions

Nevertheless, as a law professor it is part of my job to make students latter day sophists. That is, starting in the first year of law school students are taught critical legal thinking requires you to be able to understand and argue your position on behalf of your client and at the same time know and understand and be able to argue the opposing counsel's argument in order to defeat that argument. This was the way of the original sophist philosophers.

In my first year Criminal Law course we spend part of the first three weeks learning to argue both sides of a case via an exercise concerning sentencing. At the sentencing of a convicted criminal both the prosecution and the defense can argue for a certain sentence within the guidelines the legislature has mandated. These arguments are called "allocution." The prosecutor always goes first and, usually, seeks a jail or prison sentence. The defense then allocutes for a lesser sentence or even probation. However, both sides must base their sentence recommendations on a set of utilitarian guidelines that are called the "goals of sentencing," which are defined as, general deterrence, specific deterrence, incapacitation, and reform.

The student's first role is prosecutor. Each are given facts of a true case currently in the news where there was a conviction at the trial. The students are made to write out their allocution argument and read it in class. At the next class, the script is flipped and the students are made defense attorneys who must write out their argument for a lesser sentence on behalf of the defendant and read it in class. Both sides must make their allocution using the goals of sentencing. It is an interesting process and helps students learn how to argue both sides of an argument.

The Ancient Romans

The Republic of Rome had written codes of civil and criminal law three centuries before the birth of Christ. Just as Latin is still taught in some of our colleges and Universities, Roman law courses are still taught in a few American law schools. When the ancient Romans conquered new territories they always created a new capital town based on the Roman model. They would build structures and temples to their gods around a planned town square, or forum, as they called it. The first building erected was a courthouse. Inscribed over the entrance to all Roman courthouses were the words, *Nulla Poena Sine Lege,* which in Latin means, "There can be no punishment without a written law." This sentiment has been revived in modern American Jurisprudence. We can only punish people when there is written law drafted by a legislature. Judges in our country are not allowed to make judge-made law.

Did you know that in ancient Rome Julius Caesar was a lawyer, and reputedly a good one, before he became a noted general and made himself the Emperor of Rome in about the year 45 B.C.E. Caesar mixed law, war, conquest, and politics but it did not end well for him. Caesar was assassinated in the Senate in 44 B.C.E. by his political enemies. Yet, lawyering appears to be a good career if you wish to enter American politics. You may know our two houses of Congress have many lawyers. The U.S. House of Representatives is comprised of 435 Representatives and 159 of them (36%) hold law degrees. In the Senate 54 of the 100 Senators (54%) hold law degrees. Our sixteenth President of the U.S., Abraham Lincoln was a lawyer. In the twentieth Century our 42nd President, Bill Clinton, was a lawyer and now in the twenty-first century Barack Obama, the 44th President of the United States, is also a lawyer.

Law Schools

Were there law schools of old? The answer is clearly no! In the sweep of history, the creation of law schools is a rather new phenomenon. Until about 1870 would-be lawyers apprenticed in the offices of older lawyers for three to seven years before they had enough experience to handle clients and cases on their own. The push to provide legal education in a school started in about 1872 when the President of Harvard University decided it was time the University had a law school.

In that year, the President of Harvard University coaxed a young and well-respected Wall Street lawyer to come to Cambridge and become the Dean of the new school. The Dean had the unlikely name of Christopher Columbus Langdell. Dean Langdell is now considered the father of the modern day law school. Over the years he hired a law faculty and collected written opinions on a number of different law subjects and put them together in books that Langdell dubbed "Casebooks." Students would learn the law not by merely apprenticing but by actually reading and analyzing the opinions written by appellate court judges and opinions of the justices of the U.S. Supreme Court. The law professors developed a "Socratic" method or what is sometimes called the "case method" of questioning and challenging law students by pulling information out of them that leads the students to critical thinking. Nowadays law schools still rely on casebooks and the case method of teaching law. Dean Langdell retired in the early 1900's. Today, the largest building on the campus of Harvard Law School is the library – it is named Langdell Hall in honor of the first Dean.

Chapter Two
Why Apply to Law School?

I have been out of law school for several years. About half of those years were devoted to legal practice and diplomatic work and the other half has been devoted to teaching law, writing, and working with admission issues at my law school. I am proud to say I have had a great career and have found both joy and prestige at being a member of the legal profession. For me, law school was a great choice that I hope some of you will make.

Who applies to law school?

Several prospective students have asked me over the years what type of person should go to law school. There is no good answer to that question because people go to law school for a variety of reasons. Some seek a legal education to have a profession where they can be their own boss, others believe it might be a profession in which you can earn a good deal of money, while others hope to use their legal degree as a way to work in the judicial or political field. I could go on but I think you get the idea. There is no single undergraduate major that will completely prepare you for law school. I have helped train lawyers, many of whom whose undergraduate majors were in diverse field such as, anthropology, biology, chemistry, criminal justice, engineering, finance, music, philosophy, political science, sociology, and zoology.

The best law students know what kind of law they would like to practice. Often, such students have worked as a paralegal in a law office, or have been in law enforcement, or have worked in the corporate world. Very often their experience in these fields have made them realize they can use their training as a springboard into a lucrative law career. Most of these students do go on to have very successful careers. However, some of these students come to law school with a vision and mid-way through law school realize they are interested in another aspect of law. Usually, they are successful because they have found passion in the new vision. I have seen students enter law school hoping to pursue personal injury work but find they really love criminal law work.

The worst law students, and those that probably should not be in law school, are those who seek the education because their parents or other relatives have forced or cajoled them into entering law school. Often, these students find a way to flunk out, or drop out of school and ultimately find other fields of study for which they are better suited. On the other hand, several lawyers whose fathers and/or mothers were lawyers have successfully followed them into the family practice.

Having stated this, I believe a solid legal education will allow the individual the flexibility to use education in several different ways over his or her career. In my own career, I started out with a big corporate law firm where I handled insurance company defense work. After, I was recruited into the U.S. State Department where I had the opportunity to practice overseas diplomatic work. Later still, I transferred to the U.S. Department of Justice and for five years was a federal prosecutor in Washington, D.C. and for one year in the U.S. Virgin Islands. When I left government service, I had my own law practice for ten years where I specialized in criminal defense work and political asylum work. While in private practice, I was often invited to give legal commentary on television and radio concerning legal cases in the news. My career may not be your career, but having a solid legal education can open many doors to you. However, you must find your own way to make a legal education profitable and satisfying.

A few students have asked me how I decided to go to law school and pursue a legal career. For me, it started in second grade. I believe I was about seven-years-old. My elementary school consisted of eight grades; and at the end of the school year there was an eighth-grade graduation. After which, the graduates would go on to high school. Any Students above first-grade was allowed to attend the graduation. I was fascinated by the eighth-grade Valedictorian who made a short speech to the entire graduation assembly. I was impressed and realized that I, too, someday would like to be out in front of people addressing a crowd who lingered on my words. The next year, when I was eight-years-old, my mother told me I was a bright young boy with a pleasing personality. She told me I was so bright I could grow up, go to Harvard and become a diplomat. At eight I didn't know what Harvard was nor what being a diplomat meant. Nevertheless, I kept those thoughts in my head as I grew up and attended college where I learned that one of the best ways to talk to groups of people and/or become a diplomat was to go to law school. Ultimately, I fulfilled my mother's wishes by growing up, going to Harvard Law School, and, for at least part of my career, serving as diplomat with the U.S. State Department. Sometimes, mothers' words of encouragement really do work.

Rigorous Training

Law school provides rigorous training. There are several classes to attend, an enormous amount of reading, writing, and discussions of issues, concepts and cases. If you are not suited to voluminous reading, to a good deal of writing, and/or debating issues, a law school education may not be for you. On the other hand, if you like to solve puzzles, or enjoy counseling and advocating on behalf of others, or who enjoys being in leadership positions, lawyering may be for you. This advice is aimed at both young women and men interested in going to law school. The American Bar Association (ABA) recently published statistics revealing that the ratio of law school graduates for the last few years have been 47% women and 53% men. Law has truly become an equal opportunity profession.

The Bar Examination

Before leaving this chapter on applying to law school, you should also consider the Bar Examination. A three-year legal education is rigorous, but graduating from law school with a Juris Doctor (JD) degree will not by itself allow you to be a legal, licensed practitioner. First, you must take a Bar Examination and pass it. The Bar Examination is a two-day test offered at the end of February and July, with most applicants taking the summer test because it falls shortly after graduation. In most states, one of the two days is devoted to essay and multiple choice questions concerning laws of that state. The second day is known as the Multistate Bar Examination, a multiple choice exam which is the same for all states and tests common courses such as Constitutional law, criminal law, criminal procedure, evidence civil procedure, torts and commercial law.

Reciprocity / Pro Hac Vice

Each state has its own Bar Association and its own Bar Examination, which means students must study the laws of their state to pass the examination. Lawyers may practice only in the state or states where they are members of the bar in good standing. Some states may admit a lawyer to the Bar of that state if the lawyer has been admitted to the bar of another state and has practiced law for a certain number of years. This is known as admission based on "reciprocity." Courts may also grant temporary bar admission to out of state lawyers for the duration of a specific case. This is called admission *"Pro Hac Vice,"* and means admission for this one case. Several states require law students to register with the board of bar examiners before graduation, or, in some cases, immediately upon enrollment in law school if they intend to practice in those states.

Thus, if you do choose to apply to law school, it is wise to check out the Bar admission requirements for those states in which you want to practice. All states accept graduation from an American Bar Association (ABA) approved law school as meeting the state's education requirement for eligibility to sit for the bar examination. The State of California has two or three law schools not approved by the ABA. Graduates of these law schools may sit for the California Bar exam, but for no other state bars. If students pass the California Bar examination, they may practice law only in the state of California.

Chapter Three
Critical Things You Need to Know About Applying to Law School

Choosing a Law School

How do you go about choosing a school? There are approximately 215 ABA-approved law schools in the United States and Canada. The prevailing wisdom may be to choose at least three law schools. One pick may be your dream school – a Harvard, Yale, or Stanford. Usually, these schools have the most difficult admission standards and cost the most to attend. Other private law schools almost, but not quite beyond your grasp, might be Notre Dame or Georgetown Law. Then there are safe schools like your state law school with much lower tuition rates which, as a state resident, you may have the most realistic chance for admission. Nevertheless, there are several competitive private and state law schools to which you might apply.

Research Websites

Research specific law schools that interest you. Most law schools have a website. Such websites should have advice about the school's admission office, which can provide information about the school and your chances of admission.

Many Colleges and Universities have a pre-law advisor. The pre-law advisor provides reliable information about which law school fits your personal profile. The pre- law advisor may also tell you which law schools have accepted students from your college or university and provide you with an overview of the admitted student's credentials.

Law School Forums

Every fall Law School Forums organized by the Law School Admission Council (LSAC) provide opportunities to speak with law school representatives from around the country in one central location in a hotel or exhibit hall.

Law School Forums are usually held in Atlanta, Boston, Chicago, Los Angeles, Miami, New York City, San Francisco, Toronto, and Washington, D.C. Many forums feature workshops about the Law School Admission Test (LSAT), the admission process, and the legal profession that students have found helpful in making decisions about what schools to send applications.

Most law schools encourage you to visit. Many schools have programs where currently enrolled students give you a tour of the campus and answer questions about the school. Also, the ABA's website has internet links to all ABA-approved law schools.

Law School Admission Council

I mentioned the Law School Admission Council. If you plan to go to law school, you should be aware the Law School Admission Council (LSAC) is a nonprofit corporation that provides products and services to ease the admission process for law schools and their applicants. Founded in 1947, LSAC is best known for administering the Law School Admission Test (LSAT) with approximately 100,000 tests administered annually at testing centers around the world. LSAC also processes academic credentials for an average of 60,000 law school applicants each year.

Every prospective law school applicant must take the LSAT. The exam is a half-day, standardized test administered four times each year at designated testing centers around the world. The test is an integral part of the law school admission process. The test helps law schools make admission decisions by providing a standard measure of acquired reading and verbal reasoning skills essential for success in law school.

The Credential Assembly Service (CAS) helps simplify law school admission by allowing applicants to have all transcripts, recommendations, and evaluations sent only once to LSAC. The LSAC summarizes and combines that information with LSAT scores and writing samples into a report that is sent upon request to the law school to which the applicant applies. The Candidate Referral Service (CRS) makes it possible for law school candidates to provide information about themselves that make it easy for law schools to recruit them

Law schools may seek out potential applicants on the basis of specific characteristics such as undergraduate major, ethnicity, law school preferences, and other variables. Several potential applicants are recruited by law schools they might not otherwise have considered.

LSAC provides for diversity initiatives. That is, programs and initiatives are created and funded to increase the number of lawyers from racial and ethnic groups, the LGBT community, and others underrepresented in the legal profession. Through these efforts, LSAC seeks to ensure that legal education and the profession is as inclusive as possible.

More on the LSAT

The LSAT test is an integral part of the law school admission process. The test consists of five 35-minute sections of multiple choice questions. Four of the five sections contribute to the test taker's score. The unscored section typically is used to pretest new test questions or new test forms. The placement of this section will vary. A 35-minute, unscored writing sample is administered at the end of the test. Copies of the student's writing sample are sent to all law schools to which they apply.

The LSAT is designed to measure skills considered essential for success in law school: the reading and comprehension of complex texts with accuracy and insight; the organization and management of information and the ability to draw reasonable inferences from it; the ability to think critically; and, the analysis and evaluation of the reasoning and arguments of others. There are three multiple choice question types on the LSAT:

1. Reading comprehension questions measure the ability to read with understanding and insight examples of lengthy and complex materials similar to those commonly encountered in law school.

2. Analytical reasoning questions measure the ability to understand a structure of relationships and to draw logical conclusions about that structure.

3.   Logical reasoning questions assess the ability to analyze, critically evaluate, and complete arguments as they occur in ordinary language.

To register for the LSAT or CAS, you must establish or log into her or his LSAC.org account. The fees set out below are accurate at the time of writing in 2016 but may change over time. All fees are in U.S. dollars.

Basic & Auxiliary Fees

LSAT - $175

Credential Assembly

Service (CAS) - $170

Late Registration - $90

Test Center Change - $90

Test Date Change - $90

For online registrants, LSAC accepts the following forms of payments: VISA MasterCard, American Express, and Discover credit cards.

Your LSAT Score

Few people achieve their full potential on the LSAT without preparation. You can take a practice test, including the writing sample, under actual time constraints which will help estimate how much time you can afford to spend on each question as well as which question types you should practice. Free official prep material may be found at

http://www.lsac.org/jd/lsat/preparing-for-the-lsat.

Your LSAT score is based on the number of questions answered correctly, this is your "raw score." There is no deduction for wrong answers, nor are individual questions on the various test sections weighed differently. The raw scores are converted to an LSAT scale that ranges from 120 to 180. A 120 is the lowest possible score you can receive while 180 is the highest score. A score of 120 will not get you into law school. This score indicates the applicant did little more than write his or her name on the test. 180 scores are rare. However, scores in the high 170's will probably get you admitted to almost every law school in the U.S. Many Law School admission committees look favorably on applicants who have LSAT scores between 150 and 160. If an applicant takes the LSAT more than once, LSAC will average the scores earned. There is no limit on the number of times you may take the LSAT.

Students may verify or contest the machine scoring of their LSAT answer sheet and may request the sheet be hand scored. Having said this, students should also know the LSAT compare favorably with admission tests used in other graduate and professional schools. Although the LSAT score is an important part of your law school application, it is only one of several factors law schools consider with respect to admission decisions. The admission committees I have had the honor to sit on, and have sometimes chaired, look at other qualities of the candidates that might contribute to success in law school including motivation, past accomplishments, and leadership skills.

Predictive Factors for Success

In determining whom to admit, most admission committees look at a variety of factors that are most predictive of success in law school; the two factors that are objective and applicable to all candidates are the LSAT score and prior academic performance. In recent years, some schools have put less reliance on the LSAT and have given more weight to other factors. LSAC has published the criteria that may be considered by law school admission committees. These criteria certainly have been used by my school's admission committees. They include:

1. Undergraduate grade-point average
2. LSAT score
3. Undergraduate course of study
4. Graduate school work, if any
5. College attended

6. Improvement in grades and grade distribution
7. College curricular and extracurricular activities
8. Ethnic/Racial background
9. Individual character and personality
10. Letters of recommendations/evaluations
11. Writing skills
12. Personal statement or essay
13. Work experience or other post graduate experiences
14. Community service activities
15. Motivation to study and reasons for deciding to study law
16. State of residency
17. Obstacles that have been overcome
18. Past accomplishments and leadership

Several years ago, when I was the Chair of my first admission committee, the committee was confronted with making a decision on an older student who was a married father with two children and the owner of a small, family run insurance business. The applicant had a poor LSAT score and the committee was split down the middle on accepting or rejecting. I, thought he would be a good choice. I took the case to the Dean of Law School and suggested we invite the applicant to the school for a personal interview with the Dean and myself.

The applicant agreed to the interview and we spent over an hour speaking with him. In that hour we learned he was born the fifth child out of ten children of a Jamaican family. After high school he won a scholarship to a Christian College in the U.S. He did well and graduated college, married an American citizen, and became a legal permanent resident of the United States, and ultimately became a naturalized U.S. citizen. He and his wife started an insurance company five years before his application to law school. The business was going well, but he believed being a lawyer would help his business.

After his interview, both the Dean and I believed this candidate had the wherewithal to become a good lawyer. He seemed to have vision and had accomplished a great deal in life. I took what we learned to the committee which then unanimously voted to admit him. The applicant entered the law school, did well, and graduated.

He used his law degree to help his insurance business but after three years he became an Assistant District Attorney. He rose through the ranks of the office and became a chief of section. The end of the story? Two years ago this alumnus called and asked if he could speak to me at the law School. He advised me he was now running for a judgeship. I was proud of him and glad we voted to admit him despite his poor LSAT score. He had continued to accomplish quite a bit – so much so I made a $50 contribution to his campaign for judge. This young man had the vision and drive to succeed - and did, beyond his own expectations.

Chapter Four
Your Application Specifics

Once you have decided to apply to law school LSAC, I suggest you set up your LSAC.org account. This will provide a gateway to the law school admission process. Your LSAC account number will be your primary identifier for all LSAC services.

Your Application

Law schools have a variety of application requirements and deadlines that you must meet to be considered for admission. Your LSAC account will allow you to use a detailed calendar with reminders for important deadlines. Registering for the LSAT is the beginning of the process for most applicants. If you have an LSAC account, you will automatically receive your LSAT score by email about three weeks after taking the test. You should schedule your LSAT date so there will be plenty of time to obtain your score before any of your law school applications are due.

As mentioned earlier, LSAC's Credential Assembly Service (CAS) aids the admission process because you only need to have your transcripts, recommendations, and evaluations sent just one time to LSAC, where they summarize them and combine them with your LSAT scores and writing samples into a report that is sent to prospective law schools. Here are some reminders that might simplify your application process:

1.   Confirm that all information in your LSAC file is correct and current. If there is an error, correct it as soon as possible in writing.

2.   Use the same form of your name on all documents and communications with LSAC.

3.   Carefully review all documents sent to you by LSAC.

4.   Maintain and keep copies of all law school application records throughout the admission cycle and law school because some state bar associations inquire about the law school admission records of those seeking admission to the bar.

5.   Ethical conduct is expected and required in all your interactions with LSAC and law schools. Misconduct in the admission process may lead to serious consequences.

Financial Aid

A legal education is expensive but should be considered a serious investment in your future. LSAC prompts the prospective student to consider the ramifications of a large expenditure on legal education. A realistic assessment of why you are seeking a legal education and how you will pay for it is critical. The cost of a law school education could exceed $150,000. Tuition can range from a few thousand dollars a year at a state law school to more than $50,000 a year at some of the top tier law schools. Tuition today at many private law schools hovers in the $33,000 a year range. When calculating the total cost of attending law school, you must include the cost of housing, food, books, transportation, health care, and personal expenses.

A majority of law students rely on education loans as their primary, but not exclusive source of financial aid for law school. Of course, these loans must be paid back out of future income – the more you borrow – the longer the debt will have an impact on your life after graduation. The best information about financing a legal education is the financial aid office of any LSAC-member law school.

Federal student loans offer the most flexible repayment options and provide more opportunities for payment relief than loans funded by private or institutional sources. Private and institutional sources may be available but are usually used by students who are not eligible for federal student loans. The amount and types of loan funding you are eligible to borrow will be determined by the financial aid staff at the school you attend based on cost of attendance at that school, federal regulations, and institutional policies. When borrowing for law school, borrow the minimum amount needed to attend the law school of your choice. Borrow federal loans first and avoid private student loans if possible.

Scholarships, grants, and fellowships are available but on a limited basis. Some schools offer part-time employment through the Federal Work-Study Program to students in their second and third year of law school. First year law students are not expected to work so they can concentrate fully on their school work. Students who must work during their first year are encouraged to work no more than 20 hours per week.

Graduate and professional school students are considered financially independent of their parents for the purpose of determining federal eligibility. This means that for the purpose of applying for federal aid, submission of parental information is not required. The law school financial aid office will notify you of financial eligibility once all application materials have been received and processed, and if you have been admitted to the school.

You may be eligible for several different types of aid, such as scholarships which might be available based on your LSAT score and your law school grades that may bring the cost of attending law school within reach. The amount of aid you receive in each category will depend on your own resources, current federal regulations, and the financial aid policies and resources of each law school.

Diversity

All U.S. law schools recognize that minority group members have been under-represented in the legal profession. The law school population, as well as the legal profession itself, does not reflect the growing racial and ethnic population of the U.S. In an effort to promote diversity, the ABA has required all law schools to actively seek qualified African American, Hispanic, Asian, and Native American students, as well as other students of color. The ABA and those who teach law understand diversity within the classroom enriches the learning process of all students.

Law schools consider your ethnic or racial status to be whatever you indicate on your LSAT registration forms. Of course, this factor alone does not guarantee admission to a law school, but it aids admission committees in acquiring a more complete picture of the candidate. Since most law schools seek diversity in their student body, it is up to the candidate to show or explain how his/her race or ethnicity will contribute to the richness of the law school education of every student. One way to do so is to research and determine the diversity goals of the school or schools you want to send an application.

The concept of diversity is broader than ethnicity, and ethnicity is not the same as adversity. Your ethnicity is not the only way in which you can add to the diversity of the law school students. Your entire life history, sincerely told, may capture the attention of the admission committee.

Law schools do not apply different admission criteria to minority applicants. Instead, most law schools take race or ethnicity into account as one of many factors in a whole file review of candidates. Admission committee members recognize that every applicant may offer something distinctive to an entering class. I know this because I have sat on admission committees for years. Aside from LSAT scores and undergraduate GPAs, our committee members will scrutinize strong letters of recommendation or candidates' personal statements, work experience, and leadership traits. All these are factors in determining whether the applicant would be a good fit for our particular law school.

Chapter Five
A look Inside of Law School

What to expect

ABA-approved law schools usually require three years of full time study to earn the JD degree. Schools with a part-time program require four years of part-time study to earn the degree. The first year of law school may well be the most important of your law school career because you will experience a new language and a new way of learning. LSAC recognizes the first year of law school will be exciting for many and anxiety provoking for most. You will be expected to be prepared for every class, yet, in most courses, grades will be determined primarily from one examination administered at the end of the semester.

Study Groups

The professor may not provide feedback until the final examination. As a result, students need to figure out what is important in the course. A good way to do this is to form a "study group" with two or three other students that meets every week or so to determine the most important concepts the Professor is conveying. In essence, much of the first year of law school is learning how to figure things out. Often there are no clear cut yes or no answers like there may have been during your undergraduate education. How you answer legal questions, particularly in the first year of law school, depends upon how well students argue the relevant law. Some students have a difficult time when they realize, after several years of schooling there may be no one exact right answer on certain law school exam essay questions, instead you will be graded on how well you spot issues and how you argue the law and facts of the question.

First Year Curriculum

Most first year classes are dedicated to the "case method" described earlier where students focus on underlying principles that shape the law's approach. The case method, of course, involves reading and studying a number of related judicial opinions that describe an area of the law. The case method assumes the primary purpose of law school is to teach you to think like a lawyer. One of the reasons for this approach to legal education is our common law tradition where the law is constantly evolving and changing.

The first year curriculum normally includes subjects that have evolved from the common law and are the subjects most often examined on the bar examination. They are:

1. Criminal law – the basic themes of substantive criminal law, including criminal responsibility and punishment, the significance of act, intent, causation and result, as well as justification and result.

2. Contracts – the nature of enforceable promises and rules for determining appropriate remedies in case of nonperformance.

3. Civil procedure – the process of civil adjudication in the U.S., including jurisdiction and standing to sue, motions and pleadings, pretrial procedure, and the structure of civil trials.

4. Property law – concepts, uses, and historical developments in the treatment of land, buildings, natural resources, and personal objects

5. Torts – private wrongs such as negligence, assault and defamation that violate obligations of law.

6. Legal writing – research and writing component of most first year programs; requires

students to research and write memoranda concerning various legal problems. In many law schools, legal writing classes require students to participate in a moot court exercise in which they write a legal brief and are required to make an appellate oral argument of a hypothetical case.

After the First Year

Some law schools have a few required courses during the second year that are tested on the bar examination such as Constitutional Law, Commercial Law, and Evidence Law. Many law schools also require students to take a course in Professional Responsibility (Ethics). Nevertheless, in all law schools students are allowed to choose from a number of "elective courses" which might be helpful to their legal interests including, administrative law, aviation law, corporations, disability law, healthcare law, family law, immigration law, international law, labor law, maritime law, wills and estates, and many others. Most law schools also include in their elective courses clinical programs, internships, and externships which provide experiential learning. A number of U.S. law schools have summer programs abroad where students can enroll in courses devoted to comparative and international law.

Starting in the first year, student organizations supplement classroom learning. Normally, these organizations are dedicated to advancing the interests of particular groups of law students, such as BLSA (Black Law Student Association), HLSA (Hispanic Law Student Association), and the Women Law Students Association. Other student organizations are devoted to certain areas of law, including the Environmental Law Society, the Thomas More Society, Trial Team, and Moot Court as well as various sports clubs. In all U.S. law schools there is Law Review Society wherein students manage and edit most of the legal profession's principal scholarly journals. Since selection is based on outstanding academic performance during the first year, membership on the editorial staffs of such journals is considered a mark of academic distinction.

Chapter Six
Tips for Succeeding in Law School

It has been said a law career may provide an opportunity to effect change on an individual level and by representing the interest of a single client, and on a global level, by setting policy or establishing precedent in the governmental or business arenas. I certainly agree with this notion because in my career I have had the opportunity to do both. Legal educators know that by having attended law school you have become a "value-added" person. By this I mean in law school you spend at least three years learning to think critically, read broadly, and debate forcefully. These skills are worthwhile in most everything you do in our society.

Lawyers are Central to Democracy

The LSAC states that lawyers are central figures in the life of our democratic country. We are reminded that lawyers may deal with major courtroom cases or minor traffic disputes, they may work for corporations or small businesses, they may represent the impoverished or the wealthy, work in large law firms or work for themselves to effect change in our society.

To succeed as a lawyer, I believe specific character traits need to be developed and reinforced. The most valuable among them are truth and honesty if you, as a lawyer are not truthful and honest you will not have many clients and the ones you have will soon leave you. Other traits successful lawyers must have are courage, vision, perseverance, and the ability to be thorough in their work. With these traits you will go a long way as a lawyer. Without them you will be an "also ran," a person who never quite makes it and blames others for his/her lack of success. We have all seen this type of individual in other professions. For me, it is saddest to see lawyers in this condition. Why? Because to a great degree what you make of your law career is up to you. Lawyers have to make things happen. They must learn to meet people and get their name known in the community, do good work and you will be rewarded with an abundance of clients and legal business. Sit and wait for success to come magically come to you will only bring you misery.

A Lawyer Statistical Report

Many lawyers develop expertise in one field; others may be solo practitioners – and a jack of all trades. According to the ABA Foundations 2005 Lawyer Statistical Report, updated in January 2012:

- 75 percent of U.S. lawyers are in private practice; of these
  - o 62 percent work as solo practitioners or in offices of 5 or fewer lawyers,
  - o 18 percent work in offices of between 6 and 50 lawyers, and
  - o 20 percent work in firms of more than 50 lawyers.
- 7.5 percent of the profession work for government agencies
- 8.5 percent work in private industries and associations as salaried lawyers or as managers.
- 1 percent work for legal aid or as public defenders.
- 1 percent work in legal education.
- 2.5 percent work in the judiciary.
- 4.4 percent are retired or inactive.

Lawyering Skills

The practice of law is unique to the individual and no one has ever been able to describe or define the "typical lawyer." Every lawyer works with a wide variety of clients with different legal problems. However, certain basic legal skills are required of all lawyers. Learning these skills begins during your law school training and the skills are continually honed each year you practice law. Here is the list of these most important skills:

- Lawyers must be adept at both "Reading and Listening";
- Lawyers must "Analyze" legal issues in light of the existing state law or federal law and relevant policy considerations;
- Lawyers must be able to "Synthesize" material in light of the fact that issues are multifaceted and require the combination of diverse elements into a coherent whole;
- Lawyers must "Advocate" the views of groups and individuals within the context of the legal system;
- Lawyers must provide intelligent "Counsel" on the law's requirements;
- Lawyers must "Write and Speak" clearly; and
- Lawyers must "Negotiate" effectively.
-

A Law Degree for other Careers

The LSAC often reminds us that a legal education is excellent preparation for other careers, because the course of study provides a framework for organizing knowledge and teaches an analytical approach to problems. Any of the previously mentioned skills are useful for graduates who do not choose to practice law, but gravitate to something else. I have personally seen several graduates successfully pursue professions like real estate, government, education, law librarianships, business, construction, insurance, politics, and banking. Thus, law school does not train you for any particular kind of law, but rather acts as a catalyst that enables you to take advantage of various professional opportunities.

The First Job

For those who do wish to practice law, landing your first job is often a difficult hurdle. The reason for this is many students graduate from law school without a concrete vision of what kind of law career or path they would like to pursue. Remember, your first job after law school will not likely be your lifelong job. For those students smart enough to have made "Law Review" I always encourage them to land a clerkship with a judge – either state or federal. To seek a clerkship the Career Service Office at your law school will assist you. The application process should start near the end of your second year in law school. Obtaining a clerkship is competitive. Good grades, good writing skills, and extracurricular activities such as Trial Team, Moot Court, or internships on your resume help.

For students who say they would like to be trial lawyers, I encourage them to pursue work as a public defender or get experience in the State Attorney's office. In my opinion, the knowledge gained in either of these organizations is valuable. Neither of these positions pay a great entering salary, but in two or three years you will have gained a tremendous amount of knowledge about trial work and how our system of justice administration works, as well as getting to know the judges, law clerks, police officers, court reporters, and others that make our criminal justice system work. Knowing such people will aid you in becoming a better professional.

Immigration Law

Since I teach Immigration Law, among other courses, I often encourage my former students to seek work with small immigration firms, but I also advise them that working for one of the Department of Homeland Security (DHS) immigration branches will provide valuable knowledge that might be helpful if you wish to one day set up your own immigration law firm.

A recent graduate I taught immigration law had worked her way through her undergraduate degree as a paralegal at an immigration law firm. Within six months of graduation, she had set up her own law practice.

DHS Employment

The DHS branches law graduates may seek to work for are: U.S. Citizenship and Immigration Services (USCIS), U.S. Immigration and Customs Enforcement (USICE), and the U.S. Customs and Border Protection (USCBP). All of these organizations have websites that sometimes advertise job opportunities. Having worked for the U.S. State Department, I know these organizations always have a need for trained lawyers. However, it may take up to a year of background checks and clearance to obtain such jobs. Start seeking government positions early during the second semester of your second year of law school.

Personal Injury

Several graduates will gravitate toward personal injury work because it can be very profitable. Quite a few students who had been paralegals in personal injury firms while in law school have become partners in the same personal injury firms they worked for while in school.

Lawyers Online

We are in an emerging digital world that connects lawyers and their computers to other people and businesses all over the globe. I believe there will be a need for lawyers who understand the developing technology of this era who can take advantage of the intellectual property requirements of this new digital world by obtaining copyrights, trademarks, and other types of registrations for global businesses that have not yet come into existence. Yes, there will always be opportunities for and a need for lawyers.

I should add that graduating law school, passing the Bar Exam, and being sworn into the state's bar association makes you a licensed professional who may set up his or her own practice from day one. Usually these graduates know what they want to practice and want to be their own boss. All they need are clients. As a result they must market themselves and join organizations, and make themselves known throughout the community. In this day and age every lawyer needs to have a website and a footprint on social media – Facebook, a blog, a twitter account and so forth. Some work other part time jobs while getting their practice up and running. However, with perseverance that first client you successfully represent will tell two other people about you and one client may turn into three, three clients into six and six clients turn into…I think you get the picture.

Conclusion

A law school education may provide you with a career that will always be in demand and provide you with professional esteem that may make you a leader in your community. It is good to research specific law schools you might wish to attend by reviewing their websites and attend Law School Forums organized by the LSAC. Many colleges and universities have prelaw advisors who may provide you with reliable information about law schools that might fit your personal profile.

Once you have decided to apply to law school set up your LSAC account which is your gateway to the law school admission process. Your LSAC account number will be your primary identifier for all LSAC services. Your account will allow you to register for the LSAT. You should prepare yourself for the LSAT by taking advantage of the free preparation material provided at

http://www.lasc.org/jd/lsat/preparing-for-the-lsat.

The Credential Assembly Service at LSAC will simplify your law school admission by allowing to have your transcripts, recommendations and evaluations sent only once to LSAC. LSAC will summarize and combine that information with your

LSAT score that is sent to each law school you wish to apply. A law school education is expensive. You will find the best information about financing your legal education is through the financial aid office of the law school you choose to attend. I hope this book has make it easier for you to understand the application process that will allow you to go to law school and make it easier to accomplish your goal. I wish good luck to your making it into law school.

I hope that all who read my words herein go on to have a successful legal career that provides you with pride, prestige, and joy.

THE END

Glossary

AALS: The Association of American Law Schools is a nonprofit association of 179 law schools. The mission of AALS is to uphold and advance excellence in legal education by promoting the core values of excellence in teaching and scholarship, academic freedom and diversity while seeking to improve the legal profession.

ABA: The American Bar Association is a voluntary professional organization of attorneys with nearly 40,000 members. It is committed to serving its members, improving the legal profession, eliminating bias, and enhancing diversity, and advancing the rule of law throughout the U.S and the world.

ABA-APPROVED LAW SCHOOLS: The ABA is the accrediting body for law schools in the U.S. through its Section on Legal Education. The section provides the rules and procedures for accrediting law schools. A total of 205 institutions are ABA-approved which means that the J.D degree graduates of these schools can sit for the Bar Examination in any State in the U.S.

BAR EXAMINATION: In order to be licensed to practice law in any state law graduates need to take a professional licensing test known as the Bar Examination. This is a two day examination that tests the standards and knowledge needed to represent clients. Each state has its own bar examination and lawyers may only practice in states where they are members of the bar. The exam is offered each year at the end of February and July.

B.C.E.: This means a historical period before the Christian era began in 1 A.D.

CAS: The Credential Assembly Service aids law school admission by allowing applicants to have all transcripts, recommendations, and evaluations sent only once to the Law School Admission Council.

CRS: The Candidate Referral Service makes it possible for law school candidates to provide information about themselves that will make it easy for law schools to recruit them.

CASEBOOK: Law books used in teaching students how to read and analyze appellate cases that teach the rules and principles of American law.

CASE METHOD: The teaching method in law schools using casebooks.

LAWYERING SKILLS: The basic skills all lawyers must have mastered in order to counsel and represent clients. The most important skills are reading and listening, followed by other such skills as writing, speaking clearly, advocating the views of one client, and the ability to negotiate on behalf of clients.

LGBT: Those law school candidates who may consider themselves Lesbian, Gay, Bisexual or Transgendered.

LSAC: The Law School Admission Council is a nonprofit corporation founded in 1947 which provides products and services to ease the admission process of law schools. The Council is best known for administering the LSAT.

LSAT: The Law School Admission Test is a half-day standardized test administered four times a year that all law school applicants must take. The test assists law schools in making sound admission decisions by providing a standard measure of acquired reading and verbal reasoning skills that are needed in law school.

LSAT SCORE: An applicant's LSAT score is based on the number of questions answered correctly on the exam – this is the raw score. The raw score is converted to an LSAT scale that ranges from 120 to 180, with 120 being the lowest possible score and 180 the highest possible score.

USCIS: United States Citizenship and Immigration Services, Department of Homeland Security created in 2003 provides the principal services for immigration and naturalization, including refugee and asylum matters.

USICE: United States Immigration and Customs Enforcement, Department of Homeland Security. Created in 2003, this department provides investigations, detention and removal of noncitizens, and provides trial lawyers who represent the government in immigration court.

USCBP: United States Customs and Border Protection, Department of the Homeland Security. Created in 2003, this department provides for border inspection functions and border patrol.

Suggested Reading / Reference

1L of a Ride
Andrew J. McClurg (Thompson/Reuters, 2009)

Written by a law school professor that provides a beginning-to-end roadmap of what to expect the first year, focusing on practical advice about academic and emotional success.

Law School without Fear: Strategies for Success
Marshall & Helene Shapo (3d Edition 2009)

Written by two lawyers for their son before he entered law school, this light-hearted book provides practical advice and useful information about the law school experience.

Succeeding in Law School
Herbert N. Ramy (Carolina Academic Prcss, 2006)

Mindful of the rigorous learning environment new law students face, this book is a useful tool for helping students to get the most out of their abilities.

Starting Off Right in Law School

Carolyn J. Nygren (Carolina Academic Press, 1997)

Introduces basic legal concepts, vocabulary, and analysis in the context of one hypothetical case, putting the law school experience in context and giving guidance to help students balance their academic, personal, and social lives.

Mastering the Law School Exam

Suzanne Darrow-Kleinhaus (Thompson-West, 2007)

Designed to provide students with a knowledgeable, reasonable, and rational voice to navigate the intricacies of law school exams. This book is practical rather than theoretical, and provides excellent examples of how to approach a law school exam that students may use throughout their law school career.

About the Author

Professor Birdsong received his J.D. from the Harvard Law School and his B.A. from Howard University. He teaches law in Orlando, Florida.

After graduation from law school he worked four years at the law firm of Baker Hostetler. He then entered into a varied and distinguished career in government service. He served as a diplomat with the U.S. State Department with various postings in Nigeria, Germany and the Bahamas.

Professor Birdsong later served as a federal prosecutor. After leaving government service, and before he began teaching, Professor Birdsong was in private law practice in Washington, D.C.

www.BirdsongsLaw.com

lbirdsong@barry.edu

Ordering Information

New books coming soon!

Dear Reader,

If you liked this book, I would greatly appreciate you writing me a review on Amazon or any other book site.

I look forward to sharing more funny stories with you in future books.

Thank you, I really appreciate your help.

Regards,

Professor Birdsong

Winghurst Publications
1969 S. Alafaya Trail / Suite 303
Orlando, FL 32828-8732
www.BirdsongsLaw.com
lbirdsong@barry.edu

Other Books by Professor Birdsong:

* Professor Birdsong's 147 Dumbest Criminal Stories: Florida.

* 177 Dumbest Criminal Stories – International.

* Professor Birdsong's 157 Dumbest Criminal Stories.

* Professor Birdsong's Weird Criminal Law Stories.

* Professor Birdsong's "365" Weird Criminal Law Stories for Every Day of the Year.

* Professor Birdsong's Weird Criminal Law Stories, Volume 2: Stories From Around the States and Abroad.

* Professor Birdsong's Weird Criminal Law Stories, Volume 3: Stories from New York City and the East Coast.

* Professor Birdsong's Weird Criminal Law Stories - Volume 4: Stories from the Midwest.

* Professor Birdsong's Weird Criminal Law Stories, Volume 5: Stories from Way Out West.

* Professor Birdsong's Weird Criminal Law Stories - Volume 6: Women in Trouble.

* Professor Birdsong's Weird Criminal Law - Volume 6: Women in Trouble!

* Immigration: Obama must act now!

* Professor Birdsong's 77 Dumbest Criminal Stories.

* Professor Birdsong's Dumbest: Thugs, Thieves, and Rogues.

* Professor Birdsong's LAW SCHOOL GUIDE: Techniques for Choosing, and Applying to Law School

Leonard Birdsong

www.ingramcontent.com/pod-product-compliance
Lightning Source LLC
Chambersburg PA
CBHW070810210326
41520CB00011B/1899